1,98

MOTH

MOTH AT REST

BUTTERFLY

BUTTERFLY
AT REST

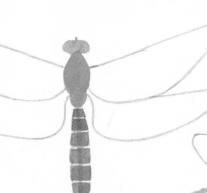

DRAGONFLY

MAYFLY

DAMSELFLY

HORNET

WASP

BEE

FLY

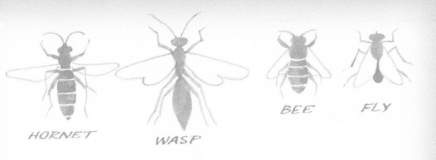

THIS NATURE NOTEBOOK BELONGS TO:

_____

_____

_____

ANT

TERMITE

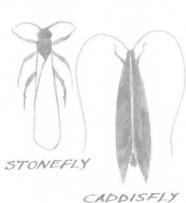

STONEFLY

CADDISFLY

CRANEFLY

MOSQUITO

GNAT

NOTE : ACTUAL SIZES WILL VARY GREATLY FROM SPECIES TO SPECIES.

Library of Congress Cataloging-in-Publication Data
Arnosky, Jim.
Bug hunter / by Jim Arnosky.
p. cm. — (Jim Arnosky's nature notebooks)
SUMMARY: Presents tips on finding and observing various bugs,
with blank pages provided for keeping records.
ISBN 0-679-86719-8
1. Insects—Juvenile literature. [1. Insects.
2. Nature study.] I. Title. II. Series: Arnosky, Jim.
Jim Arnosky's nature notebooks.
QL467.2.A77 1997 595.7'00723—dc20 96-21649

Printed in the United States of America 10 9 8 7 6 5 4 3 2 1

JIM ARNOSKY'S
NATURE NOTEBOOKS
BUG HUNTER

Random House New York

BUG HUNTING

If you cannot let a butterfly flutter by without following it a little ways, if you have ever spent time watching a spider weave its web, if you find ants, beetles, caterpillars, and dragonflies fascinating—then you are a born bug hunter!

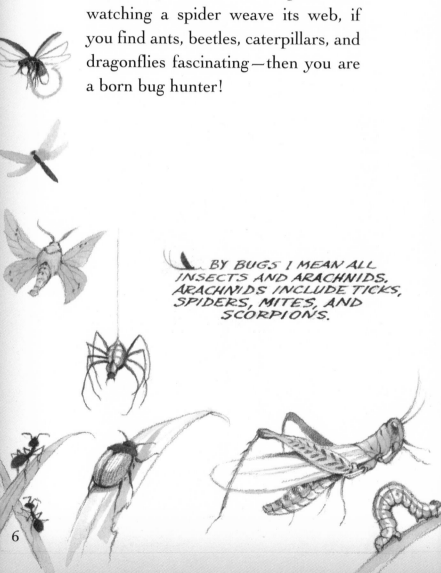

BY BUGS I MEAN ALL INSECTS AND ARACHNIDS. ARACHNIDS INCLUDE TICKS, SPIDERS, MITES, AND SCORPIONS.

Anywhere you look outdoors you are likely to see some bug flying or crawling around. But real bug hunting begins when you go out to find and watch a certain species, such as a special butterfly or a particular caterpillar.

MONARCH
BUTTERFLY
AND
MONARCH
CATERPILLAR

7

BUG HUNTING— INDOORS

There are bugs to look for indoors too. Spiders make webs in skyscraper windows. Houseplants are home to tiny flies, mites, spiders, earwigs, aphids, and ants. Occasionally a ladybug may be discovered climbing a green leaf of a potted plant or scaling window glass. I once found a daddy-longlegs in our bathtub!

LADYBUG ON HOUSEPLANT

IDENTIFYING BUGS

Exactly how many different kinds of bugs there are in the world is unknown. We do know that there are more insects on earth than all other kinds of animals combined. But even with so many different kinds of bugs, the basic types are easy to recognize.

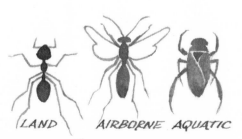

LAND   AIRBORNE AQUATIC

THE SILHOUETTE CHARTS AT THE BEGINNING AND END OF THIS BOOK WILL HELP YOU QUICKLY IDENTIFY MOST TYPES OF BUGS.

BUG-HUNTING EQUIPMENT

Unlike birds and other wildlife, bugs are not shy. They will crawl or fly all around you. In warm seasons, we may actually have to cover ourselves with repellent to keep bugs away. I've done some of my best bug watching streamside, observing mayflies close-up that have alighted on my sleeve or hand.

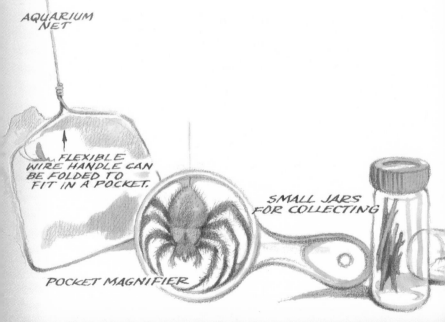

AQUARIUM NET

FLEXIBLE WIRE HANDLE CAN BE FOLDED TO FIT IN A POCKET.

SMALL JARS FOR COLLECTING

POCKET MAGNIFIER

For viewing tiny bugs afield, I carry a pocket magnifying lens. A small aquarium net comes in handy for gently scooping up aquatic insects for a closer look. Another piece of bug-hunting equipment you might consider is a small plastic jar in which to carry home pieces of wings, shed insect skins, or even dead insects you find. You may also want to carry a pair of tweezers to pick up these small and often delicate things. Found objects and specimens are fascinating to examine close-up with a magnifying lens or a microscope. When viewed through the microscope, even the tiniest fly looks monstrous!

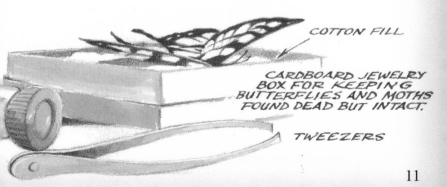

COTTON FILL

CARDBOARD JEWELRY BOX FOR KEEPING BUTTERFLIES AND MOTHS FOUND DEAD BUT INTACT.

TWEEZERS

USING A BINOCULAR

In the field, a 7 x 35 binocular can bring you closer to large insects such as butter-flies and dragonflies, without your having to chase after them. A binocular is the only safe way to get a close-up view of stinging scorpions, hornets, and biting ants. Never get closer than 12 feet to an ant mound, unless you are sure the ants are not the biting kind. Stay well away from any place you suspect to be a beehive or hornets' nest. Whenever I see one of these stinging insects flying in a straight line, I stop in my tracks and watch where it is heading. Then I head in the opposite direction.

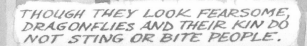
THOUGH THEY LOOK FEARSOME, DRAGONFLIES AND THEIR KIN DO NOT STING OR BITE PEOPLE.

BUG HUNTING— IN GARDENS

BALD-FACED HORNET

The best place to hunt bugs is in a garden. Any garden of flowers or vegetable plants attracts scores of flies, beetles, ants, spiders, caterpillars, and butterflies. By midsummer, when the plants are at their tallest, grasshopper populations explode. Every step you take sends one or two grasshoppers jumping.

PAPER WASP

YELLOW JACKET

HONEY BEE

LEARN WHICH BUGS IN YOUR AREA DO STING OR BITE AND AVOID THEM. ABOVE ARE FOUR OF THE MOST COMMON.

13

TICKS

When I'm bug hunting in tall plants or grasses, I'm always careful about ticks. I stay to the edges of the greenery and walk only on short, mowed grass. If you do not rub up against a plant a tick happens to be on, the tick cannot climb on you. Ticks are easier to spot on light-colored clothing. Cover your skin with long sleeves and pants, and tuck the bottom of your pants into your socks. Be aware of the possibility of tiny ticks in your yard or garden, and if you happen to brush against tall grasses or weeds, stop and check your clothes for the presence of ticks. Carefully remove them using a pointed twig or the tweezers in your bug-hunting gear before they migrate to your skin. The

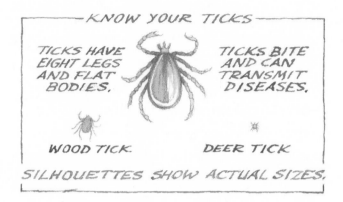

KNOW YOUR TICKS

TICKS HAVE EIGHT LEGS AND FLAT BODIES.

TICKS BITE AND CAN TRANSMIT DISEASES.

WOOD TICK

DEER TICK

SILHOUETTES SHOW ACTUAL SIZES.

tick must come off intact. Never squeeze, crush, or break a tick, exposing its bodily fluids. Some ticks carry diseases that can be transmitted to humans.

WHEN WALKING IN TALL GRASS OR WEEDS, TUCK YOUR PANTS INTO YOUR SOCKS AS A PRECAUTION AGAINST TICKS.

RECORDING FINDINGS

Most of the smaller bugs you find can be sketched and written up on one page of your notebook. Recording larger insects may take two pages. First record the identity of each subject. If you know the proper name (i.e., DRAGONFLY), write it down. If you are not certain exactly what a bug's name is, write down what you think it is—a fly, beetle, caterpillar, and so on. Next record the location and whether the bug was seen on the ground, a stone, a blade of grass, or a flower, or simply hovering in air. Draw all bugs life-size, even if you have to use most of two pages to do it. Be sure to add every detail you can see—segmented abdomens, jointed legs, wing veining, antennae, and body bristles or hairs.

AUGUST 10, 1995

CRINKLE COVE
LAKE CHAMPLAIN

DRAGONFLY

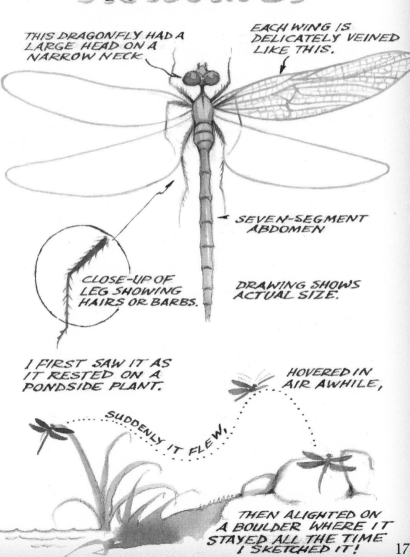

THIS DRAGONFLY HAD A LARGE HEAD ON A NARROW NECK.

EACH WING IS DELICATELY VEINED LIKE THIS.

SEVEN-SEGMENT ABDOMEN

CLOSE-UP OF LEG SHOWING HAIRS OR BARBS.

DRAWING SHOWS ACTUAL SIZE.

I FIRST SAW IT AS IT RESTED ON A PONDSIDE PLANT.

SUDDENLY IT FLEW,

HOVERED IN AIR AWHILE,

THEN ALIGHTED ON A BOULDER WHERE IT STAYED ALL THE TIME I SKETCHED IT!

17

YOUR NATURE NOTEBOOK

Your nature notebook is small and flexible so you can roll it up, put it in a pocket, and carry it wherever you go. But as small as it may be, it can hold many wonderful experiences. Take care to write small and fit a lot on every page. Be sure to read all you can find about every insect you record in your notebook. This way you will increase your knowledge. Study pictures and photographs of your field subjects and copy them to add more details to your field sketches.

I'll be dropping in on a few more pages throughout the rest of the book to tell you a little more about bugs. Until then...

HAPPY BUG HUNTING!

Jim Arnosky

AT NIGHT, WITHOUT LEAVING YOUR PORCH, YOU CAN ATTRACT MANY MOTHS AND OTHER NIGHT-FLYING BUGS SIMPLY BY TURNING ON A BRIGHT FLASHLIGHT.

ALSO, YOU CAN USE A FLASHLIGHT TO LOCATE SPIDER WEBS ON SHRUBS OR IN BETWEEN PORCH RAILINGS.

TRY HOLDING A FLASH-LIGHT SHINING UPWARD JUST BELOW A SPIDER'S WEB. YOU'LL SEE HOW SPARKLING THE SILKEN STRANDS OF A SPIDER WEB CAN BE.

MOTH CATERPILLARS CONSTRUCT OR SPIN VARIOUSLY SHAPED COCOONS IN WHICH TO HIBERNATE AND FOR CHANGING SLOWLY INTO WINGED MOTHS IN A PROCESS CALLED METAMORPHOSIS.

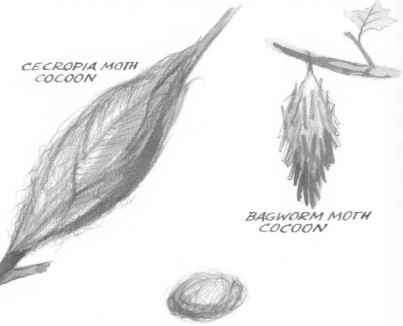

CECROPIA MOTH COCOON

BAGWORM MOTH COCOON

ISABELLA MOTH COCOON

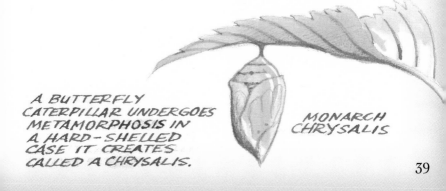

A BUTTERFLY CATERPILLAR UNDERGOES METAMORPHOSIS IN A HARD-SHELLED CASE IT CREATES CALLED A CHRYSALIS.

MONARCH CHRYSALIS

39

43

CADDIS CASES

THE LARVA OF THE CADDISFLY LIVES UNDER WATER IN SWIFT-FLOWING STREAMS.

TYPICAL CADDIS LARVA ("CADDISWORM")

CADDISFLY

SILHOUETTE SHOWS ACTUAL SIZE.

TO PROTECT THEMSELVES IN THEIR RUGGED ENVIRONMENT, CADDIS LARVAE MAKE CASES USING VARIOUS NATURAL MATERIALS.

STICK CASE

CASES MADE OF LEAF BITS

VARIOUS CASES MADE OF TINY PEBBLES

A NEAT RECTANGULAR CASE MADE OF THIN STRIPS OF LEAVES

THE CADDIS CASES ARE TRULY MOBILE HOMES, AS THE CADDIS LARVAE DRAG THEIR CASES FROM PLACE TO PLACE.

NOTE: CADDIS CASES ARE FOUND IN WATER LESS THAN 1' DEEP. NEVER WADE DEEPER THAN 1' IN SWIFT WATER.

ABOUT THE AUTHOR

Naturalist Jim Arnosky has written and illustrated over 35 nature books for children. His titles have earned numerous honors, including American Library Association Notable Book Awards and Outstanding Science Books for Children Awards presented by the National Science Teachers Association Children's Book Council Joint Committee. He has also received the Eva L. Gordon Award for Body of Work for his contribution to children's literature.

An all-around nature lover, Mr. Arnosky can often be found fishing, hiking, boating, or videotaping wildlife on safari. He lives with his family in South Ryegate, Vermont.

GRUB

CATERPILLAR

MEALYBUG

EARWIG

WALKINGSTICK

MANTID

WEEVIL

VARIOUS BEETLE SHAPES

COCKROACH

CICADA

GRASSHOPPER

CRICKET

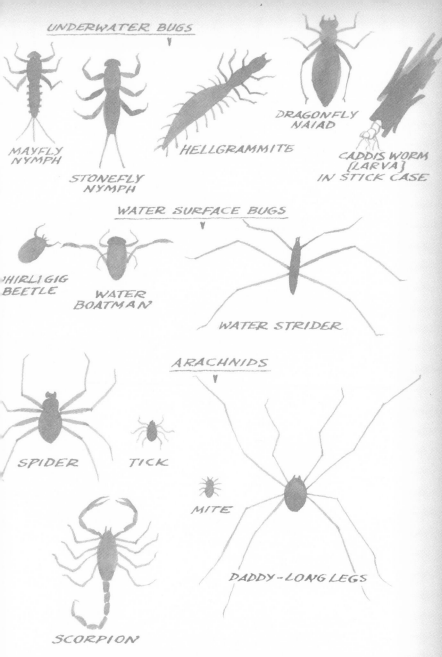

UNDERWATER BUGS

MAYFLY NYMPH

STONEFLY NYMPH

HELLGRAMMITE

DRAGONFLY NAIAD

CADDIS WORM [LARVA] IN STICK CASE

WATER SURFACE BUGS

WHIRLIGIG BEETLE

WATER BOATMAN

WATER STRIDER

ARACHNIDS

SPIDER

TICK

MITE

DADDY-LONG LEGS

SCORPION

NOTE: ARACHNIDS HAVE EIGHT LEGS.
TRUE INSECTS HAVE SIX LEGS.